family favorites
chicken

Bath · New York · Singapore · Hong Kong · Cologne · Delhi · Melbourne

chicken, cheese & arugula salad

ingredients

SERVES 4

5$\frac{1}{2}$ oz/150 g arugula leaves

2 celery stalks, trimmed
and sliced

$\frac{1}{2}$ cucumber, sliced

2 scallions, trimmed
and sliced

2 tbsp chopped
fresh parsley

1 oz/25 g walnut pieces

12 oz/350 g boneless roast
chicken, sliced

4$\frac{1}{2}$ oz/125 g Stilton cheese,
cubed

handful of seedless
red grapes, cut in
half (optional)

salt and pepper

dressing

2 tbsp olive oil

1 tbsp sherry vinegar

1 tsp Dijon mustard

1 tbsp chopped
mixed herbs

method

1 Wash the arugula leaves, pat dry with paper towels, and put them into a large salad bowl. Add the celery, cucumber, scallions, parsley, and walnuts and mix together well. Transfer onto a large serving platter. Arrange the chicken slices over the salad, then scatter over the cheese. Add the red grapes, if using. Season well with salt and pepper.

2 To make the dressing, put all the ingredients into a screw-top jar and shake well. Alternatively, put them into a bowl and mix together well. Drizzle the dressing over the salad and serve.

red chicken salad

ingredients

SERVES 4

4 boneless chicken breasts

2 tbsp red curry paste

2 tbsp vegetable or peanut oil

1 head Napa cabbage,
    shredded

6 oz/175 g bok choy, torn into
    large pieces

$^1/_2$ savoy cabbage, shredded

2 shallots, chopped finely

2 garlic cloves, crushed

1 tbsp rice wine vinegar

2 tbsp sweet chili sauce

2 tbsp Thai soy sauce

method

1 Slash the flesh of the chicken several times and rub the curry paste into each cut. Cover and let chill overnight.

2 Cook in a heavy-bottom pan over medium heat or on a grill pan for 5–6 minutes, turning once or twice, until cooked through. Keep warm.

3 Heat 1 tablespoon of the oil in a wok or large skillet and stir-fry the Napa cabbage, bok choy, and savoy cabbage until just wilted. Add the remaining oil, shallots, and garlic, and stir-fry until just tender, but not browned. Add the vinegar, chili sauce, and soy. Remove from the heat.

4 Arrange the leaves on 4 serving plates. Slice the chicken, arrange on the salad greens, and drizzle the hot dressing over. Serve immediately.

thai chicken salad

ingredients

SERVES 6

vegetable oil spray

4 oz/115g skinless chicken
   breast, cut lengthwise
   horizontally

3 limes

dressing

1 tbsp finely shredded
   lemongrass

1 small green chile, finely
   chopped

3 tbsp lime juice

$1/2$-inch/1-cm galangal or
   gingerroot, peeled and
   thinly sliced into strips

$1^1/2$ tsp sugar

2 tbsp white wine vinegar

3 fl oz water

$1^1/2$ tsp cornstarch

salad

1 oz/25 g rice vermicelli

$1^3/4$ oz/50 g mixed bell
   peppers, seeded

$1^3/4$ oz/50 g carrot

$1^3/4$ oz/50 g zucchini

$1^3/4$ oz/50 g snow peas

$1^3/4$ oz/50 g baby corn

$1^3/4$ oz/50 g broccoli florets

$1^3/4$ oz/50 g bok choy

4 tbsp roughly chopped fresh
   cilantro leaves

method

1 To make the dressing, put all the dressing ingredients, except the cornstarch, into a small pan over low heat and bring to a boil. Blend the cornstarch with a little cold water, gradually add to the pan, stirring constantly, and cook until thickened. Remove from the heat and let cool.

2 Heat a grill pan over high heat and spray lightly with oil. Add the chicken and cook for 2 minutes on each side, or until thoroughly cooked through. Remove the chicken from the pan and shred.

3 To make the salad, cover the rice vermicelli with boiling water then let it cool in the water. Meanwhile, finely slice the bell peppers, carrot, zucchini, snow peas, and baby corn into strips. Cut the broccoli florets into 1/4-inch/5-mm pieces and shred the bok choy. Drain the rice vermicelli and put all the salad ingredients with the chicken into a large bowl. Pour over the dressing and toss together, making sure that all the ingredients are well coated.

4 Cover and refrigerate for at least 2 hours before serving. Serve with the juice from half a lime squeezed over each portion.

chicken in lemon & garlic

ingredients

SERVES 6–8

4 large skinless, boneless
    chicken breasts

5 tbsp Spanish olive oil

1 onion, finely chopped

6 garlic cloves,
    finely chopped

grated rind of 1 lemon, finely
    pared zest of 1 lemon and
    juice of both lemons

4 tbsp chopped fresh
    flat-leaf parsley, plus extra
    to garnish

salt and pepper

lemon wedges and crusty
    bread, to serve

method

1 Using a sharp knife, slice the chicken breasts widthwise into very thin slices. Heat the olive oil in a large, heavy-bottom skillet, add the onion and cook for 5 minutes, or until softened, but not browned. Add the garlic and cook for an additional 30 seconds.

2 Add the sliced chicken to the skillet and cook gently for 5–10 minutes, stirring from time to time, until all the ingredients are lightly browned and the chicken is tender.

3 Add the grated lemon rind and the lemon juice and let it bubble. At the same time, deglaze the skillet by scraping and stirring all the bits on the bottom of the skillet into the juices with a wooden spoon. Remove the skillet from the heat, stir in the parsley, and season with salt and pepper.

4 Transfer, piping hot, to a warmed serving dish. Sprinkle with the pared lemon zest, garnish with the parsley, and serve with lemon wedges for squeezing over the chicken, accompanied by chunks or slices of crusty bread for mopping up the juices.

soy chicken wings

ingredients

SERVES 3–4

9 oz/250 g chicken wings,
    defrosted if frozen

8 fl oz/250 ml/1 cup water

1 tbsp sliced scallion

1-inch/2.5-cm piece of fresh
    gingerroot, cut into
      4 slices

2 tbsp light soy sauce

$1/2$ tsp dark soy sauce

1 star anise

1 tsp sugar

method

1 Wash and dry the chicken wings. In a small pan, bring the water to a boil, then add the chicken, scallion, and gingerroot and bring back to a boil.

2 Add the remaining ingredients, then cover and simmer for 30 minutes.

3 Using a slotted spoon, remove the chicken wings from any remaining liquid and serve hot.

five-spice chicken with vegetables

ingredients

SERVES 4

2 tbsp sesame oil

1 garlic clove, chopped

3 scallions, trimmed
and sliced

1 tbsp cornstarch

2 tbsp rice wine

4 skinless chicken breasts,
cut into strips

1 tbsp Chinese
five-spice powder

1 tbsp grated fresh gingerroot

4 fl oz/125 ml/$^{1}/_{2}$ cup
chicken stock

3$^{1}/_{2}$ oz/100 g baby corn cobs,
sliced

10$^{1}/_{2}$ oz/300 g/3 cups
bean sprouts

finely chopped scallions,
to garnish, optional

freshly cooked jasmine rice,
to serve

method

1 Heat the oil in a preheated wok or large skillet. Add the garlic and scallions and stir-fry over medium-high heat for 1 minute.

2 In a bowl, mix together the cornstarch and rice wine, then add the mixture to the pan. Stir-fry for 1 minute, then add the chicken, five-spice powder, gingerroot, and chicken stock and cook for another 4 minutes. Add the corn cobs and cook for 2 minutes, then add the bean sprouts and cook for another minute.

3 Remove from the heat, garnish with chopped scallions, if using, and serve with freshly cooked jasmine rice.

chicken satay

ingredients

SERVES 4

2 tbsp vegetable or peanut oil

1 tbsp sesame oil

juice of $1/2$ lime

2 skinless, boneless chicken
breasts, cut into small cubes

dip

2 tbsp vegetable or peanut oil

1 small onion, chopped finely

1 small fresh green chile,
seeded and chopped

1 garlic clove, chopped finely

4 oz/115 g/$1/2$ cup crunchy
peanut butter

6–8 tbsp water

juice of $1/2$ lime

method

1 Combine both the oils and the lime juice in a nonmetallic dish. Add the chicken cubes, cover with plastic wrap, and let chill for 1 hour. Soak 8–12 wooden skewers in cold water for 30 minutes before use, to prevent burning.

2 To make the dip, heat the oil in a skillet and sauté the onion, chile, and garlic over low heat, stirring occasionally, for about 5 minutes, until just softened. Add the peanut butter, water, and lime juice and let simmer gently, stirring constantly, until the peanut butter has softened enough to make a dip—you may need to add extra water to make a thinner consistency.

3 Meanwhile, drain the chicken cubes and thread them onto the wooden skewers. Put under a hot broiler or on a barbecue, turning frequently, for about 10 minutes, until cooked and browned. Serve hot with the warm dip.

sweet-&-sour chicken

ingredients

SERVES 4–6

1 lb/450 g lean chicken meat, cubed

5 tbsp vegetable or peanut oil

1/2 tsp minced garlic

1/2 tsp finely chopped fresh gingerroot

1 green bell pepper, coarsely chopped

1 onion, coarsely chopped

1 carrot, finely sliced

1 tsp sesame oil

1 tbsp finely chopped scallion

freshly cooked rice, to serve

marinade

2 tsp light soy sauce

1 tsp Shaoxing rice wine

pinch of white pepper

1/2 tsp salt

dash of sesame oil

sauce

8 tbsp rice vinegar

4 tbsp sugar

2 tsp light soy sauce

6 tbsp tomato ketchup

method

1 Place all the marinade ingredients in a bowl and marinate the chicken pieces for at least 20 minutes.

2 To prepare the sauce, heat the vinegar in a pan and add the sugar, light soy sauce, and tomato ketchup. Stir to dissolve the sugar, then set aside.

3 In a preheated wok or deep pan, heat 3 tablespoons of the oil and stir-fry the chicken until it starts to turn golden brown. Remove and set aside.

4 In the clean wok or deep pan, heat the remaining oil and cook the garlic and gingerroot until fragrant. Add the vegetables and cook for 2 minutes. Add the chicken and cook for 1 minute. Finally add the sauce and sesame oil, then stir in the scallion and serve with rice.

lime chicken with mint

ingredients

SERVES 6

3 tbsp finely chopped
   fresh mint

4 tbsp honey

4 tbsp lime juice

salt and pepper

12 boneless chicken thighs

mixed salad, to serve

sauce

5 fl oz/150 ml/^{2}/$_3$ cup
   lowfat thick plain yogurt

1 tbsp finely chopped
   fresh mint

2 tsp finely grated lime rind

method

1 Mix the mint, honey, and lime juice in a large bowl and season with salt and pepper. Use toothpicks to keep the chicken thighs in neat shapes and add the chicken to the marinade, turning to coat evenly.

2 Cover with plastic wrap and let the chicken marinate in the refrigerator for at least 30 minutes. Remove the chicken from the marinade and drain. Set aside the marinade.

3 Preheat the broiler to medium. Place the chicken on a broiler rack and cook under the hot broiler for 15–18 minutes, or until the chicken is tender and the juices run clear when the tip of a knife is inserted into the thickest part of the meat, turning the chicken frequently and basting with the marinade.

4 Meanwhile, combine all the sauce ingredients in a bowl. Remove the toothpicks and serve with a mixed salad and the sauce, for dipping.

bacon-wrapped chicken burgers

ingredients

SERVES 4

1 lb/450 g fresh ground chicken

1 onion, grated

2 garlic cloves, crushed

2 oz/55 g/³⁄₈ cup pine nuts, toasted

2 oz/55 g Gruyère cheese, grated

2 tbsp fresh snipped chives

salt and pepper

2 tbsp whole wheat flour

8 lean Canadian bacon slices

1–2 tbsp corn oil

method

1 Place the ground chicken, onion, garlic, pine nuts, cheese, chives, and salt and pepper in a food processor. Using the pulse button, blend the mixture together using short sharp bursts. Scrape out onto a board and shape into 4 even-size burgers. Coat in the flour, then cover and let chill for 1 hour.

2 Wrap each burger with 2 bacon slices, securing in place with a wooden toothpick.

3 Heat a heavy-bottom skillet and add the oil. When hot, add the burgers and cook over medium heat for 5–6 minutes on each side, or until thoroughly cooked through. Serve the burgers at once.

chicken fajitas

ingredients

SERVES 4

3 tbsp olive oil, plus extra
    for drizzling
3 tbsp maple syrup or honey
1 tbsp red wine vinegar
2 garlic cloves, crushed
2 tsp dried oregano
1–2 tsp dried
    red pepper flakes
salt and pepper
4 skinless, boneless
    chicken breasts
2 red bell peppers, seeded
    and cut into 1-inch/
    2.5-cm strips
8 flour tortillas, warmed

method

1 Place the oil, maple syrup, vinegar, garlic, oregano, pepper flakes, salt, and pepper in a large, shallow plate or bowl and mix together.

2 Slice the chicken across the grain into slices 1 inch/2.5 cm thick. Toss in the marinade until well coated. Cover and let chill in the refrigerator for 2–3 hours, turning occasionally.

3 Heat a grill pan until hot. Lift the chicken slices from the marinade with a slotted spoon, lay on the grill pan, and cook over medium-high heat for 3–4 minutes on each side, or until cooked through. Remove the chicken to a warmed serving plate and keep warm.

4 Add the bell peppers, skin-side down, to the grill pan, and cook for 2 minutes on each side. Transfer to the serving plate.

5 Serve at once with the warmed tortillas to be used as wraps.

filo chicken pie

ingredients

SERVES 6–8

3 lb 5 oz/1.5 kg whole
   chicken
1 small onion, halved,
   and 3 large onions,
   chopped finely
1 carrot, sliced thickly
1 celery stalk, sliced thickly
pared zest of 1 lemon
1 bay leaf
10 peppercorns
$5^1/_2$ oz/155 g butter
2 oz/55 g/scant $^1/_2$ cup
   all-purpose flour
5 fl oz/150 ml/$^2/_3$ cup milk
salt and pepper
1 oz/25 g/$^1/_3$ cup kefalotiri or
   romano cheese, grated
3 eggs, beaten
8 oz/225 g filo pastry (work
   with one sheet at a time
   and keep the remaining
   sheets covered with a
   damp dish towel)

method

1 Put the chicken in a large pan with the halved onion, carrot, celery, lemon zest, bay leaf, and peppercorns. Add cold water to cover and bring to a boil. Cover and simmer for about 1 hour, or until the chicken is cooked.

2 Remove the chicken and set aside to cool. Bring the stock to a boil and boil until reduced to about 20 fl oz/625 ml/$2^1/_2$ cups. Strain and reserve the stock. Cut the cooled chicken into bite-size pieces, discarding the skin and bones.

3 Fry the chopped onions until softened in 2 oz/55 g of the butter. Add the flour and cook gently, stirring, for 1–2 minutes. Gradually stir in the reserved stock and the milk. Bring to a boil, stirring constantly, then simmer for 1–2 minutes until thick and smooth. Remove from the heat, add the chicken, and season. Let cool, then stir in the cheese and eggs.

4 Melt the remaining butter and use a little to grease a deep 12 x 8-inch/30 x 20-cm metal baking pan. Cut the pastry sheets in half widthwise. Line the pan with one sheet of pastry and brush it with a little melted butter. Repeat with half of the pastry sheets. Spread the filling over the pastry, then top with the remaining pastry sheets, brushing each with butter and tucking down the edges.

5 Bake in a preheated oven, 375°F/190°C, for about 50 minutes, until golden. Serve warm.

chicken kabobs with yogurt sauce

ingredients

SERVES 4

10 fl oz/300 ml/1$\frac{1}{4}$ cups
    strained plain yogurt
2 garlic cloves, crushed
juice of $\frac{1}{2}$ lemon
1 tbsp chopped fresh herbs
    such as oregano, dill,
    tarragon, or parsley
salt and pepper
4 large skinned, boned
    chicken breasts
oil, for oiling
8 firm stems of fresh
    rosemary, optional
shredded romaine lettuce,
    to serve
rice, to serve
lemon wedges, to garnish

method

1 To make the sauce, put the yogurt, garlic, lemon juice, herbs, salt, and pepper in a large bowl and mix well together.

2 Cut the chicken breasts into chunks measuring about 1$\frac{1}{2}$ inches/4 cm square. Add to the yogurt mixture and toss well together until the chicken pieces are coated. Cover and leave to marinate in the refrigerator for about 1 hour. If you are using wooden skewers, soak them in cold water for 30 minutes before use.

3 Preheat the broiler. Thread the pieces of chicken onto 8 flat, oiled, metal kabob skewers, wooden skewers, or rosemary stems and place on an oiled broiler pan.

4 Cook the kabobs under the broiler for about 15 minutes, turning and basting with the remaining marinade occasionally, until lightly browned and tender.

5 Pour the remaining marinade into a pan and heat gently but do not boil. Serve the kabobs with shredded lettuce on a bed of rice and garnish with lemon wedges. Accompany with the yogurt sauce.

gingered chicken kabobs

ingredients

SERVES 4

3 skinless, boneless chicken
    breasts, cut into small
    cubes

juice of 1 lime

1-inch/2.5-cm piece
    gingerroot, peeled and
    chopped

1 fresh red chile, seeded
    and sliced

2 tbsp vegetable or peanut oil

1 onion, sliced

2 garlic cloves, chopped

1 eggplant, cut into chunks

2 zucchini, cut into thick slices

1 red bell pepper, seeded and
    cut into squares

2 tbsp red curry paste

2 tbsp Thai soy sauce

1 tsp jaggery or soft light
    brown sugar

boiled rice, with chopped
    cilantro, to serve

method

1 Put the chicken cubes in a shallow dish. Mix the lime, gingerroot, and chile together and pour over the chicken pieces. Stir gently to coat. Cover and let chill in the refrigerator for at least 3 hours to marinate.

2 Soak 8–12 wooden skewers in cold water for 30 minutes before use, to prevent burning.

3 Thread the chicken pieces onto the soaked wooden skewers and cook under a hot broiler for 3–4 minutes, turning frequently, until they are cooked through.

4 Meanwhile, heat the oil in a wok or large skillet and sauté the onion and garlic for 1–2 minutes, until softened, but not browned. Add the eggplant, zucchini, and bell pepper and cook for 3–4 minutes, until cooked but still firm. Add the curry paste, soy sauce, and sugar, and cook for 1 minute.

5 Serve hot with boiled rice, stirred through with chopped cilantro.

thai-style chicken chunks

ingredients

SERVES 4

4 skinless, boneless chicken
  breasts, cut into small
  chunks
freshly cooked jasmine rice,
  to serve
chopped fresh cilantro,
  to garnish

marinade

1 red chile and 1 green chile,
  seeded and finely
  chopped
2 garlic cloves, chopped
$1^3/_4$ oz/50 g chopped fresh
  cilantro
1 tbsp finely chopped fresh
  lemongrass
$^1/_2$ tsp ground turmeric
$^1/_2$ tsp garam masala
2 tsp brown sugar
2 tbsp Thai fish sauce
1 tbsp lime juice
salt and pepper

method

1 To make the marinade, put the red and green chiles, garlic, cilantro, and lemongrass into a food processor and process until coarsely chopped. Add the turmeric, garam masala, sugar, fish sauce, and lime juice, season with salt and pepper, and blend until smooth.

2 Put the chicken chunks into a nonmetallic (glass or ceramic) bowl, which will not react with acid. Pour over enough marinade to cover the chicken, then cover with plastic wrap and let chill for at least $2^1/_2$ hours. Cover the remaining marinade with plastic wrap and let chill until the chicken is ready.

3 When the chicken chunks are thoroughly marinated, lift them out, and grill them over hot coals for 20 minutes, or until cooked right through, turning them frequently and basting with the remaining marinade. Arrange the chicken on serving plates with some freshly cooked jasmine rice. Garnish with chopped fresh cilantro and serve.

grilled chicken with lemon

ingredients

SERVES 4

4 chicken fourths

grated rind and juice of
    2 lemons

4 tbsp olive oil

2 garlic cloves, crushed

2 sprigs fresh thyme, plus
    extra to garnish

salt and pepper

method

1 Prick the skin of the chicken fourths all over with a fork. Put the chicken pieces in a dish, add the lemon juice, oil, garlic, thyme, salt, and pepper, and mix well. Cover and let marinate in the refrigerator for at least 2 hours.

2 To cook the chicken, preheat the barbecue or broiler. Put the chicken on the barbecue grill or in a broiler pan and baste with the marinade. Cook for 30–40 minutes, basting and turning occasionally, until the chicken is tender. (To test if the chicken is cooked, pierce the thickest part of the chicken pieces with a skewer. If the juices run clear, it is ready.) Serve hot, garnished with thyme sprigs and the grated lemon rind.

traditional roast chicken

ingredients

SERVES 4

1 oz/25 g butter, softened

1 garlic clove,
    finely chopped

3 tbsp finely chopped
    toasted walnuts

1 tbsp chopped
    fresh parsley

salt and pepper

1 oven-ready chicken,
    weighing 4 lb/1.8 kg

1 lime, cut into fourths

2 tbsp vegetable oil

1 tbsp cornstarch

2 tbsp water

lime wedges and fresh
    rosemary sprigs,
    to garnish

roast potatoes and a selection
    of freshly cooked
    vegetables, to serve

method

1 Mix 1 tablespoon of the butter with the garlic, walnuts, and parsley together in a small bowl. Season well with salt and pepper. Loosen the skin from the breast of the chicken without breaking it. Spread the butter mixture evenly between the skin and breast meat. Place the lime fourths inside the body cavity.

2 Pour the oil into a roasting pan. Transfer the chicken to the pan and dot the skin with the remaining butter. Roast in a preheated oven, 375°F/190°C, for 1³/₄ hours, basting occasionally, until the chicken is tender and the juices run clear when a skewer is inserted into the thickest part of the meat. Lift out the chicken and place on a serving platter to rest for 10 minutes.

3 Blend the cornstarch with the water, then stir into the juices in the pan. Stir over low heat until thickened, adding more water if necessary. Garnish the chicken with lime wedges and rosemary sprigs. Serve with roast potatoes and a selection of freshly cooked vegetables and spoon over the thickened juices.

tuscan chicken

ingredients

SERVES 4

2 tbsp all-purpose flour

salt and pepper

4 skinned chicken quarters
    or portions

3 tbsp olive oil

1 red onion, chopped

2 garlic cloves, chopped finely

1 red bell pepper, seeded and
    chopped

pinch of saffron threads

5 fl oz/150 ml/⅔ cup chicken
    stock or a mixture of
    chicken stock and dry
    white wine

14 oz/400 g canned
    tomatoes, chopped

4 sun-dried tomatoes in oil,
    drained and chopped

8 oz/225 g portobello
    mushrooms, sliced

4 oz/115 g/⅔ cup black
    olives, pitted

4 tbsp lemon juice

fresh basil leaves, to garnish

tagliatelle, fettuccine, or
    tagliarini and crusty bread,
    to serve

method

1 Place the flour on a shallow plate and season with salt and pepper. Coat the chicken in the seasoned flour, shaking off any excess. Heat the olive oil in a large, flameproof casserole. Add the chicken and cook over medium heat, turning frequently, for 5–7 minutes, until golden brown. Remove from the casserole and set aside.

2 Add the onion, garlic, and red bell pepper to the casserole, reduce the heat and cook, stirring occasionally, for 5 minutes, until softened. Meanwhile, stir the saffron into the stock.

3 Stir the tomatoes, with the juice from the can, and the sun-dried tomatoes, mushrooms, and olives into the casserole and cook, stirring occasionally, for 3 minutes. Pour in the stock and saffron mixture and the lemon juice. Bring to a boil, then return the chicken to the casserole.

4 Cover and cook in a preheated oven, 350°F/180°C, for 1 hour, until the chicken is tender. Garnish with the basil leaves and serve immediately with pasta and crusty bread.

chicken kiev

ingredients

SERVES 4

4 tbsp butter, softened

1 garlic clove, finely chopped

1 tbsp finely chopped fresh
parsley

1 tbsp finely chopped fresh
oregano

salt and pepper

4 skinless, boneless chicken
breasts

3 oz/85 g fresh white or
whole wheat bread
crumbs

3 tbsp freshly grated
Parmesan cheese

1 egg, beaten

9 fl oz/250 ml vegetable oil,
for deep-frying

slices of lemon and flat-leaf
parsley sprigs, to garnish

freshly cooked new potatoes
and selection of cooked
vegetables, to serve

method

1 Place the butter and garlic in a bowl and mix together well. Stir in the chopped herbs and season well with salt and pepper. Pound the chicken breasts to flatten them to an even thickness, then place a tablespoon of herb butter in the center of each one. Fold in the sides to enclose the butter, then secure with wooden toothpicks.

2 Combine the bread crumbs and grated Parmesan on a plate. Dip the chicken parcels into the beaten egg, then coat in the bread crumb mixture. Transfer to a plate, cover, and let chill for 30 minutes. Remove from the refrigerator and coat in the egg and then the breadcrumb mixture for a second time.

3 Pour the oil into a deep-fryer to a depth that will cover the chicken parcels. Heat until it reaches 350–375°F/180–190°C, or until a cube of bread browns in 30 seconds. Transfer the chicken to the hot oil and deep-fry for 5 minutes, or until cooked through. Lift out the chicken and drain on paper towels.

4 Divide the chicken among 4 serving plates, garnish with lemon slices and parsley sprigs, and serve with new potatoes and a selection of vegetables.

chicken fricassée

ingredients

SERVES 4

1 tbsp all-purpose flour

salt and white pepper

4 skinless, boneless chicken
   breasts, about 5 oz/140 g
   each, trimmed of all visible
   fat and cut into $^{3}/_{4}$-inch/
   2-cm cubes

1 tbsp sunflower or corn oil

8 pearl onions

2 garlic cloves, crushed

8 fl oz/250 ml/1 cup
   chicken stock

2 carrots, diced

2 celery stalks, diced

8 oz/225 g/2 cups
   frozen peas

1 yellow bell pepper, seeded
   and diced

4 oz/115 g white mushrooms,
   sliced

4 fl oz/125 ml/$^{1}/_{2}$ cup lowfat
   plain yogurt

3 tbsp chopped fresh parsley

method

1 Spread out the flour on a dish and season with salt and pepper. Add the chicken and, using your hands, coat in the flour. Heat the oil in a heavy-bottom pan. Add the onions and garlic and cook over low heat, stirring occasionally, for 5 minutes. Add the chicken and cook, stirring, for 10 minutes, or until just beginning to color.

2 Gradually stir in the stock, then add the carrots, celery, and peas. Bring to a boil, then reduce the heat, cover, and let simmer for 5 minutes. Add the bell pepper and mushrooms, cover, and let simmer for an additional 10 minutes.

3 Stir in the yogurt and chopped parsley and season with salt and pepper. Cook for 1–2 minutes, or until heated through, then transfer to 4 large, warmed serving plates and serve immediately.

pasta & chicken medley

ingredients

SERVES 2

$4^1/_2$–$5^1/_2$ oz/125–150 g dried
  pasta shapes, such
  as fusilli
2 tbsp mayonnaise
2 tsp bottled pesto sauce
1 tbsp sour cream
salt and pepper
6 oz/175 g cooked skinless,
  boneless chicken
1–2 celery stalks
1 large carrot
$4^1/_2$ oz/125 g/1 cup black
  grapes (preferably
  seedless)
celery leaves, to garnish

french dressing

1 tbsp wine vinegar
3 tbsp extra virgin olive oil
salt and pepper

method

1 To make the french dressing, whisk all the ingredients together in a pitcher until smooth.

2 Bring a large, heavy-bottom pan of lightly salted water to a boil. Add the pasta, return to a boil and cook for 8–10 minutes, or until just tender but still firm to the bite. Drain thoroughly, rinse, and drain again. Transfer to a bowl and mix in 1 tablespoon of the French dressing while hot. Let stand until cold.

3 Mix the mayonnaise, pesto sauce, and sour cream together in a bowl, and season with salt and pepper. Cut the chicken into narrow strips. Cut the celery diagonally into narrow slices. Reserve a few grapes for the garnish, halve the rest, and remove any pips. Cut the carrot into julienne strips.

4 Add the chicken, celery, carrot, the halved grapes, and the mayonnaise mixture to the pasta, and toss thoroughly. Taste and adjust the seasoning, if necessary. Arrange the pasta mixture in 2 serving dishes and garnish with the reserved black grapes and the celery leaves.

chicken lasagna

ingredients

SERVES 6

2 tbsp olive oil

2 lb/900 g/4 cups fresh
ground chicken

1 garlic clove, finely chopped

4 carrots, chopped

4 leeks, sliced

16 fl oz/500 ml/2 cups
chicken stock

2 tbsp tomato paste

salt and pepper

4 oz/115 g Cheddar cheese,
grated

1 tsp Dijon mustard

20 fl oz/625 ml/2^1/$_2$ cups hot
béchamel sauce

4 oz/115 g dried no-precook
lasagna

béchamel sauce

20 fl oz/625 ml/2^1/$_2$ cups milk

1 bay leaf

6 black peppercorns

2 slices of onion

mace blade

4 tbsp butter

6 tbsp all-purpose flour

salt and pepper

wild arugula and Parmesan
shavings, to serve

method

1 To make the béchamel sauce, pour the milk into a pan and add the bay leaf, peppercorns, onion, and mace. Heat gently to just below boiling point, then remove from the heat, cover, let infuse for 10 minutes, then strain. Melt the butter in a separate pan. Sprinkle in the flour and cook over low heat, stirring constantly, for 1 minute. Gradually stir in the milk, then bring to a boil and cook, stirring, until thickened and smooth. Season.

2 Heat the oil in a heavy-bottom pan. Add the chicken and cook over medium heat, breaking it up with a wooden spoon, for 5 minutes, or until browned all over. Add the garlic, carrots, and leeks, and cook, stirring occasionally, for 5 minutes.

3 Stir in the chicken stock and tomato paste and season with salt and pepper. Bring to a boil, reduce the heat, cover, and let simmer for 30 minutes.

4 Whisk half the Cheddar cheese and the mustard into the hot béchamel sauce. In a large ovenproof dish, make alternate layers of the chicken mixture, lasagna, and cheese sauce, ending with a layer of cheese sauce. Sprinkle with the remaining Cheddar cheese and bake in a preheated oven, 375°F/190°C, for 1 hour, or until golden brown and bubbling. Serve immediately, with arugula and Parmesan shaving.

spanish rice with chicken

ingredients

SERVES 4

3 tbsp olive oil

2 lb 12 oz/1.25 kg chicken
　　pieces

salt and pepper

2 onions, sliced

6 oz/175 g/scant 1 cup
　　long-grain rice

4 fl oz/125 ml/$\frac{1}{2}$ cup
　　dry white wine

pinch of saffron threads,
　　lightly crushed

12 fl oz/375 ml/1$\frac{1}{2}$ cups
　　chicken stock

1–2 mild fresh green chiles,
　　such as serrano

2 garlic cloves, finely
　　chopped

2 beefsteak tomatoes, peeled,
　　seeded and chopped

fresh cilantro sprigs,
　　to garnish

method

1 Heat 2 tablespoons of the oil in a flameproof casserole. Season the chicken with salt and pepper, add to the casserole, and cook over medium heat, turning occasionally, for 8–10 minutes, or until golden. Transfer to a plate with a perforated spoon.

2 Add the remaining oil to the casserole. Add the onions and cook over low heat, stirring occasionally, for 5 minutes, or until translucent. Add the rice and cook, stirring, for 2 minutes, or until the grains are transparent and coated with oil.

3 Pour in the wine. Bring to a boil, then reduce the heat, cover, and let simmer for 8 minutes, or until all the liquid has been absorbed. Combine the saffron and stock and pour into the casserole. Stir in the chiles and garlic and season with salt. Cover and simmer for 15 minutes.

4 Add the tomatoes and return the chicken pieces to the casserole, pushing them down into the rice. Cover and cook for an additional 25 minutes, or until the chicken is cooked through and tender. Garnish with cilantro sprigs and serve.

This edition published by Parragon in 2008

Parragon
Queen Street House
4 Queen Street
Bath BA1 1HE, UK

Copyright © Parragon Books Ltd 2008

ISBN 978-1-4075-1878-7

Printed in China

Notes for the reader
• This book uses both imperial, metric, and US cup measurements. Follow the same units of measurement throughout; do not mix imperial and metric.
• All spoon measurements are level; teaspoons are assumed to be 5 ml and tablespoons are assumed to be 15 ml.
• Unless otherwise stated, milk is assumed to be full fat, eggs and other individual fruits such as bananas are medium, and pepper is freshly ground black pepper.
• Some recipes contain nuts. If you are allergic to nuts you should avoid them and any products containing nuts. Recipes using raw or very lightly cooked eggs should be avoided by infants, the elderly, pregnant women, convalescents and anyone suffering from an illness.